VISION DISORDERS

VISION DISORDERS

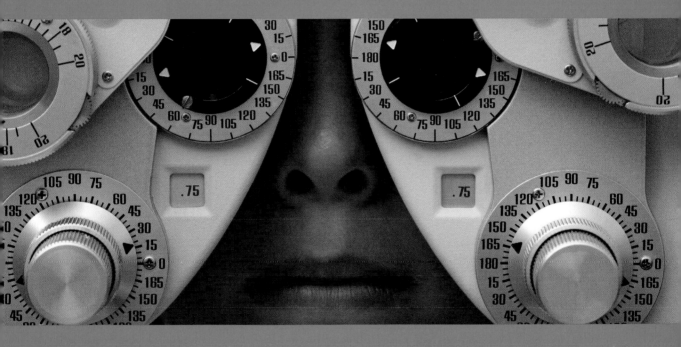

Lorrie Klosterman

 Marshall Cavendish
Benchmark
New York

With thanks to Susan B. Bressler MD, Julia G. Levy PhD Professor of Ophthalmology, at the Johns Hopkins University School of Medicine for her expert review of the manuscript.

Marshall Cavendish Benchmark
99 White Plains Road
Tarrytown, New York 10591-5502
www.marshallcavendish.us

This book is not intended for use as a substitute for advice, consultation, or treatment by a licensed medical practitioner. The reader is advised that no action of a medical nature should be taken without consultation with a licensed medical practitioner, including action that may seem to be indicated by the contents of this work, since individual circumstances vary and medical standards, knowledge, and practices change with time. The publisher, author, and medical consultants disclaim all liability and cannot be held responsible for any problems that may arise from the use of this book.

Library of Congress Cataloging-in-Publication Data
Klosterman, Lorrie.
Vision disorders / by Lorrie Klosterman.
p. cm. — (Health alert)
Includes index.
Summary: "Provides comprehensive information on the causes, treatment, and history of vision disorders"—Provided by publisher.
ISBN 978-0-7614-3982-0
1. Vision disorders—Juvenile literature. 2. Eyeglasses—Juvenile literature. 3. Eye—Juvenile literature. I. Title.
RE91.K56 2010
617.7—dc22
                         2008051247

Photo research by Candlepants Incorporated

Cover Photo: Ann Cutting / Getty Images

The photographs in this book are used by permission and through the courtesy of:
Getty Images: DEA / M. Fermariello, 3; Stock4B, 8; Nucleus Medical Art, Inc., 12, 26; Dorling Kindersley, 16, 41, 45; Ellen Martorelli, 18; 3D4Medical.com, 20; Ericka McConnell, 24; Andy Lyons, 29; Arthur Tilley, 46; Steven Puetzer, 48; Jim Cummins, 51; Brad Wilson, 52; altrendo images, 55, 56. *Alamy Images*: Phototake Inc., 13, 49; Purestock, 17; Carol and Mike Werner, 37. *Photo Researchers Inc.*: Alfred Pasieka, 5, 14; BSIP, 22; Cordelia Molloy, 32. *The Image Works*: SSPL, 35. *Corbis*: Rolf Vennenbernd/dpa, 39; Pallava Bagla, 42.

Editor: Joy Bean
Publisher: Michelle Bisson
Art Director: Anahid Hamparian

Printed in Malaysia
6 5 4 3 2 1

CONTENTS

Chapter 1   What Is It Like to Have a Vision   6
                 Disorder?

Chapter 2   What Are Vision Disorders?   10

Chapter 3   The History of Vision Disorders   34
                 and Remedies

Chapter 4   Diagnosing, Treating, and Coping   44
                 with Vision Disorders

                 Glossary   58

                 Find Out More   61

                 Index   62

WHAT IS IT LIKE TO HAVE A VISION DISORDER?

In the fourth grade, Jenna began to have trouble with her eyesight. She sat near the back of the classroom, and when the teacher wrote on the board, Jenna had trouble reading it. Whenever the students were asked to talk about the information on the board, Jenna stayed quiet.

Jenna did not tell anyone about her eyesight problem because she did not want to wear glasses. Although several of her classmates had glasses, she could not imagine having to wear them every day. One day at home, she had secretly tried on her older brother's glasses to see how she looked in them. Seeing her reflection made her even more certain she wanted nothing to do with glasses.

But soon Jenna had to take an eye test at school, like everyone else. The school nurse, who did the testing, sent a note home to Jenna's parents saying that their daughter could see things up close, but she had trouble reading letters on the eye chart, which had been 20 feet (6.1 meters) away. Jenna's mom insisted that Jenna go to an **ophthalmologist**—an eye doctor—to learn about what was causing her vision problems and to see if glasses would help.

Jenna was unhappy on the drive to the ophthalmologist's office, but she got more hopeful as soon as she walked in the door. In the waiting area she saw hundreds of pairs of glasses on display, in all shapes and sizes and colors. Everywhere there were posters of people who looked great in glasses. There were even glasses for people who had perfect vision, so they could look fashionable by sometimes wearing glasses.

When it was Jenna's turn to see the eye doctor, she was worried about the strange-looking machines the doctor would use to evaluate her eyes. But the checkup was very simple and painless. When she was asked to look at a chart—which she could not see very well—the eye doctor put different lenses in front of her eyes to find ones that would make her distance vision clear instead of blurry. For the first time, Jenna could read the eye chart with ease.

After finding the right lenses, Jenna looked for frames to hold them. She tried on dozens of them. The office's style specialist helped Jenna decide which frames looked best on her. The stylist showed her the newest fashions that other kids her age were choosing. As it turned out, Jenna liked three frames so much that she wanted them all. When she finally chose one, the lenses were put in, and she got to choose a case to protect her glasses when she was not wearing them. To her surprise, she actually now liked the idea of wearing glasses.

Jenna had two more surprises. On the drive home from the eye doctor, she wore her glasses and discovered a whole new world of things that had been just a blur before—street signs, hills in the distance, birds flying overhead, and even the sign

There are many colors and styles of eyeglasses available.

that listed what movies were playing at the local theater. She was so happy to see these things well for the first time. The final surprise was at school the next day. Classmates told her she looked great. Some of them wanted to try on her glasses. Instead of feeling bad about her looks, Jenna felt great. And she no longer had to be silent when the teacher asked questions. Even from the back of the room she could see well, and she happily joined in.

2

WHAT ARE VISION DISORDERS?

Vision is one of the body's five senses. Together with smell, sound, touch, and taste, vision allows us to understand the world around us. Of all the senses, vision is the one people rely on the most. Still, we often take vision for granted, and we do not realize how remarkable and important it is.

Many people have some sort of problem with their vision. Often, these problems occur because the eye is shaped a little differently than it should be. The eye is either too short or too long, which makes objects appear blurry. This is easily corrected with glasses or contact lenses. Other times a disease may cause damage to the eye. Aging can also lead to vision problems. Brain damage can influence vision, too. Certain vision problems are inherited from a parent, so they are present at birth. Even a person's diet can affect his or her vision.

THE AMAZING EYE

To understand what can go wrong with vision, it is important to understand how a healthy eye works. No other part of the body is quite like the eye. Like a video camera, it collects images of everything within view—near and far, moving or still, in dim or bright light. Each eye, or eyeball, is about the size of a small plum. It is filled with a clear, jellylike substance called the **vitreous humor**. An eyeball is held within a cup-shaped part of the skull called the **eye socket**. Most of the eyeball is hidden behind the eyelids.

The visible parts of the eyeball are the colored **iris**, the black **pupil** in the center of the iris, and the **sclera**—the white area surrounding the iris. The portion of the eyeball that cannot be seen is covered with white sclera, too. There are tiny blood vessels running within the clear tissue that covers the sclera. They look like tiny red, curly threads. When your eyes are irritated or you have not slept much, the blood vessels are larger, which gives your sclera a pink or red tinge.

The iris is the part that makes eyes blue, green, brown, or some color in between. The iris is made of muscles that can tighten or loosen slightly. When they do this, they change the size of the pupil. The pupil is simply a hole in the middle of the iris, that looks black because the interior of the eye is dark. As the pupil gets larger, more light can enter the eyeball. When it is smaller, less light can enter. The iris controls pupil

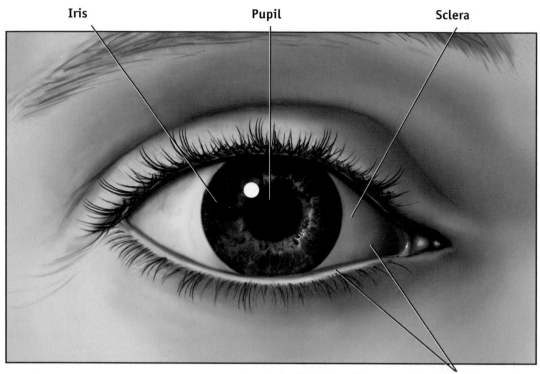

Iris   Pupil   Sclera

Conjunctive (lines eyelid and surface of eye)

The iris, pupil, and sclera are the three parts we immediately see when we look at someone's eye.

size automatically, allowing more light in when it is dark out and blocking too much light from getting in when it is very bright.

All the visible parts of the eye are covered by a very thin layer of living cells that protects it and helps keep the eye moist. The part of the layer that covers the sclera is called the **conjunctiva**. The part that covers the iris and pupil is called the **cornea**. The cornea is completely clear so that light can pass through easily.

THE LENS

Light coming into the eye first passes through the cornea, then through the pupil, and then through the transparent **lens**. The lens is clear and disc shaped, like a flattened pea. It is held in place by a ring of tiny muscles, the **ciliary muscles**, which are attached to the lens's edge like petals sticking out from the round center of a flower. The other ends of the muscles connect to the inner surface of the eyeball in a circle, just behind the iris.

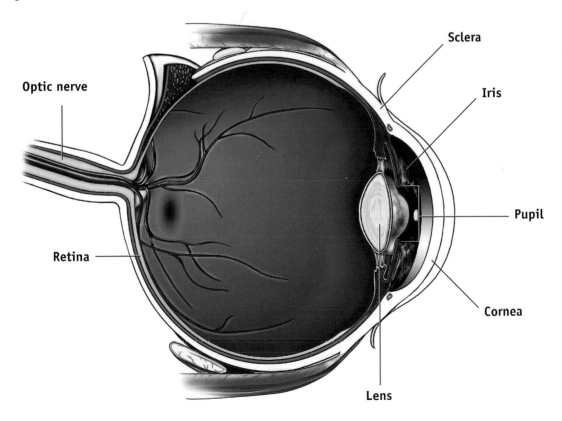

Sclera

Optic nerve

Iris

Pupil

Retina

Cornea

Lens

This illustration shows a side view cross section of a human eye.

The lens is flexible. It changes shape as the ciliary muscles tighten or relax. The shape of the lens allows us to focus on things at different distances. As people age, the elastic nature of the lens changes so that it cannot change shape as easily. As a result, people's ability to focus on nearby objects decreases. For this reason, most older people need to wear glasses when they read.

THE RETINA

Light that enters each eyeball is focused by the cornea and the lens onto the back surface of the eye (on the inside of the eyeball). That surface is called the **retina**. It is a very specialized area made of millions of cells that react to light. Two different kinds of retinal cells aid in vision. One type, called **rods** (because of their shape when viewed under a microscope), is excellent at detecting small amounts of light. Rods are especially helpful when light is dim,

This computer illustration shows the structure of the retina, with nerve fibers (top) that work together with the rods and cones (bottom half of figure) in the eye.

but they do not notice a difference in color. It is the other type of cells, the **cones**, that detects colors. Cones need plenty of light to work well. At night, colored objects look gray because the cones do not react much to the colors in dim light. Some cones respond to red color. Others respond to blue. Yet others respond to green. All light, no matter what color, is made of some combination of red, blue, and green light. Different amounts of those colors make up the hundreds of different colors our eyes can see.

Healthy rods and cones are necessary for good vision. When light hits the cells, they send many signals per second to nearby nerve cells or nerve fibers. The nerve fibers, in turn, carry the signals through the **optic nerves** toward the brain. The brain then figures out what the eyes are seeing.

An optic nerve connects each eyeball to the brain, which allows the brain to organize the information coming from each eye. An optic nerve is about as thick as a pencil. Some of the nerves carry signals about what they "see." A different group of nerves, which are not part of the optic nerve, go from the brain to the eyeballs. These nerves control eye movements and pupil size.

Eyeballs are made of living cells, just like other parts of the body. They need a continual supply of nutrients, water, oxygen, and other substances to remain healthy. These are supplied by blood vessels that run on the surface of the eyeball, within the eyeball, and behind it.

Color Blindness

The vision disorder known as **color blindness** should really be called poor color vision. A person with color blindness can see yet some of the colors look gray. The most common type of poor color vision is when certain shades of reds and of greens look gray, but sometimes the disorder involves other colors. Colors are missing because certain cone cells are not making enough of the chemicals they need to respond to light. Most cases of poor color vision are inherited, meaning that parents pass the disorder on to their children. Boys inherit poor color vision more often than girls do. Other causes of poor color vision include illness, taking certain medications, and old age.

Living with poor color vision is generally not difficult. When driving a car, for instance, it is very important to tell red from green at a traffic signal. That is easy to cope with, though, since the red light is always at the top of the traffic signal and the green light is at the bottom.

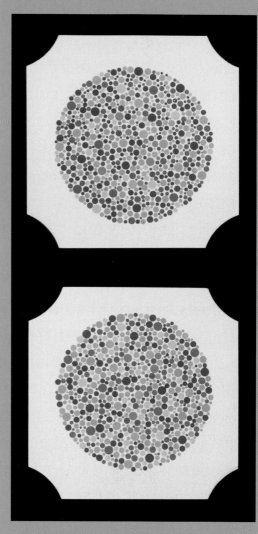

This is a common test given to find out if a person is colorblind. Can you see the numbers five and seven hidden in the dots?

HOW EYESIGHT WORKS

Light shines upon objects and then bounces off them. The bounced, or reflected, light heads off in all directions. The light travels as straight beams, like tiny flashlight beams. These beams are called light rays. The light rays travel through air and also through transparent objects such as glass, thin fabrics, plastic, water—and parts of the eye. Light passes through the eyeball's cornea, then through the pupil, and then through the lens.

Light rays that pass through the center of the lens continue straight toward the retina. But light rays near the edges of the lens are "bent" inward slightly, so they, too, arrive near the center of the retina instead of hitting its edges. The light rays bend because the lens has a curved surface instead of being flat like a glass window. Rays of light change direction a little as they pass through a curved surface.

The image that reaches the retina after passing through the lens is very tiny. Think of how large your school looks as you approach it. Its image must fit, in miniature form, on the retina, which is no

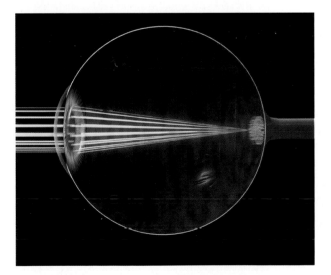

This illustration shows how light that enters the eye (left) passes thorugh the eye's cornea, pupil, and lens, and is focused on the retina.

larger than a quarter! The light-bending ability of the lens makes this possible. The cornea also bends light a bit, because it has a curved surface, too.

SEEING NEAR AND FAR

Good vision means being able to see clear, sharp images of objects no matter how near or far away they are. The lens changes shape to make this possible. A plump lens bends light more than a flatter lens. A plump lens focuses nearby objects on the retina, while a flatter lens focuses distant objects on the retina.

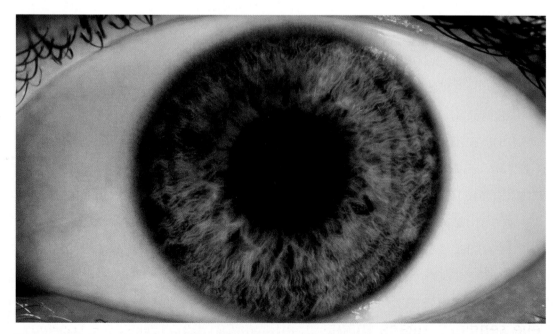

Your eyeball is constantly working for you. It is always focusing on objects in your sight so that you can see them clearly.

To see how this works, look into the distance for a minute or two and then look at a book right in front of you. It takes a moment—usually less than a second—for the words to come into sharp focus. During that time, the ciliary muscles are changing the shape of your lenses so that the book's image falls sharply into focus on your retinas.

FROM EYE TO BRAIN

An eye that makes a perfect image is said to have perfect **acuity.** But there is more to good vision than good acuity. The brain must make sense of the images. The brain learns to do this early in a person's life. The brain must learn to combine the images that come from each eye into a single image. The brain also learns how to link language and eyesight. For instance, different colors arrive at the brain as signals from different cone cells. A child learns to name these different signals as colors. The brain also learns to recognize shapes, faces, places, movements, and much more.

THREE-DIMENSIONAL VISION

For the best vision, both eyes must be looking at an object at the same time. Because the eyes are a few inches apart, their views of the world are slightly different from each other. Each eye sends its image to the brain, which then creates a three-dimensional version of what is being viewed. You can check this by looking at something close to you while covering one eye, then quickly covering the other eye instead. The object appears to jump a little from one place to another. Also, with one eye covered, the object looks a bit flat instead of three-dimensional.

EYEBALLS ON THE LOOSE?

Eyeballs cannot get knocked out and roll around the room, as many scary movies and stories suggest. Eyeballs are held securely in place in their sockets, even though they can move easily to look in many directions. The eyelids help hold eyeballs in a little, but they are not very strong. However, the base of each eyelid (the area that does not move up and down when you blink) is tightly attached to the eyeball and holds it firmly in place. The optic nerve, which connects the eyeball to the brain, also helps to anchor the eyeball in place. Finally, each eyeball has tiny muscles that move it while also helping to hold it in place. The muscles are attached at one end to the eyeball and at the other end to the bones of the eye socket.

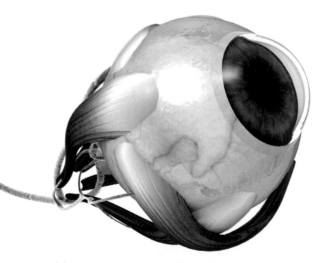

This computer illustration shows the muscles that are attached to the eyeball (red) and nerves that control them (yellow).

Even with these attachments, some people's eyes look as though they may not be held in very well because the white areas are showing a lot. That may be due to an illness that makes their eyelids open extremely wide all the time, or a different illness that causes fluid to collect behind the eyeballs and push them outward. A very serious head injury might cause an eyeball to be pushed forward from the eye socket. It may slip right back in again because of its attachments, or doctors at the emergency room may need to help settle it back in place.

BLURRY VISION

The most common problem with vision is that objects look blurry. Many people who can easily see things close up cannot see objects in the distance clearly. People with that problem are said to be **nearsighted**. The medical term for nearsightedness is **myopia**. People who have the opposite problem are said to be **farsighted**. They see faraway objects perfectly, but they cannot see nearby things clearly. The medical term for farsightedness is **hyperopia**.

Nearsightedness and farsightedness happen because the lens and the position of the retina are not working together properly. The lens must bend light rays just the right amount so the images of objects are sharp, or in focus, when they land on the retina. A lens that does not bend light rays quite

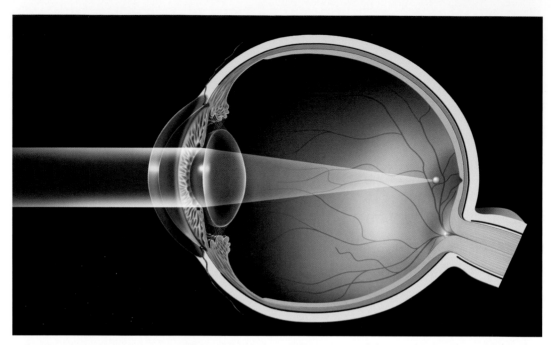

This illustration shows an eyeball that is nearsighted and cannot see things clearly in the distance. The object (green ball) is focused in front of the retina, not on it.

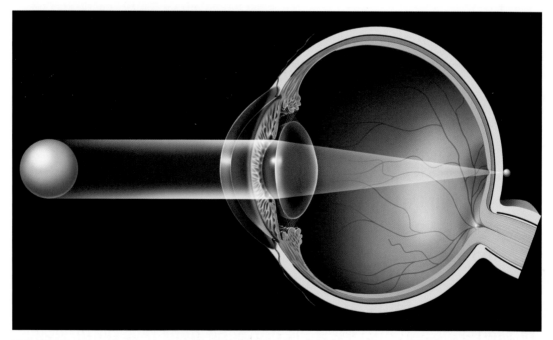

This illustration shows an eyeball that is farsighted and cannot see things clearly close up. The object is focused behind the retina.

enough, or bends them too much, creates a focused image that is in front of or behind the retina. So the image on the retina itself is blurry. Another cause of nearsightedness or farsightedness is an eyeball that is a little too short or a little too long. That puts the retina either too close to the lens or too far from it. Even if the lens bends light rays properly, as the light rays continue their journey to the retina, they strike the retina too soon or too late to be in proper focus.

ASTIGMATISM

A different kind of blurry vision is when objects that are in the center of the view are in focus but objects around the edges look blurry or oddly shaped. This problem is called **astigmatism**. The usual cause for astigmatism is a cornea that is not evenly curved. A normally shaped cornea is an important part of good eyesight because it bends light rays a little, and it works with the lens to make a good image. With astigmatism, light rays that pass through different areas of the cornea are bent different amounts. This distorts the image of an object even before it reaches the lens.

TRACKING

An important part of good vision is tracking. Tracking means that the two eyeballs move in unison to watch something. Tracking allows you to do things such as watch a running dog, view the scenery from a moving car, watch movies, or play video games. These eye movements also allow you to scan across objects that are not moving, such as the lines of print in a book or a musical score. If the two eyeballs are not moving as a team, the objects do not look right. They may be blurry, or you may see double images. Tracking is a skill that the eyes and brain learn during a person's first few years of life.

Babies are unable to control their eyes very well, but as they get older, their muscles get stronger, and they are able to focus on a single object much better.

Tracking is possible because each eyeball has six tiny, straplike muscles. One end of each muscle is attached to the side or the back of the eyeball. The other end is attached to bones of the eye socket. When a muscle contracts, or shortens, it pulls on the eyeball and turns it. When a muscle relaxes, or lengthens, it allows other muscles to pull the eyeball in the opposite direction. To turn the eyes in unison, the brain sends signals that make some muscles contract while others relax. It takes practice to

Keeping Eyes Moist

....

The conjunctiva on the eye's surface helps to keep the eye moist. It makes a small amount of liquid that coats the eye. That helps the eyelids to move easily when you blink. The moisture also nourishes the living cells of the eye's surface. Sometimes an eyelash or piece of dust gets stuck in the moisture and is hard to remove. The best-known source of eye moisture, though, is tears. These salty drops are made by tear glands. Each eye has a tear gland under the eyelid, just above the outer corner of the eye. Whenever you blink, a small amount of moisture is pulled from the tear gland across the eye.

Tear glands release a lot more fluid, though, at certain times. Everyone has felt a swell of emotion that makes the eyes water, or fill with tears. Crying is an emotional reaction to any number of feelings—not only sadness, but also joy, anger, and fear. When those feelings arise, the brain sends signals to the tear glands that make them release tears. An automatic tear-releasing trigger also happens whenever dust or a bug or an eyelash suddenly gets stuck on the eye's surface. The tears are a natural reaction that aids in washing out the offending item.

perfect this sort of eye control. Babies cannot control their eyes very well, but as they get older, and with practice watching things, their eye control gets better and very rapid.

CROSSED EYES AND AMBLYOPIA

Crossed eyes, or **strabismus**, means that the two eyes do not look in the same direction at the same time. They may both be turned inward, or one eye may look upward, downward, or outward while the other looks straight ahead. Usually the problem is that the muscles of one eye are not controlling it properly. With strabismus, each eye sends a slightly different picture to the brain. The brain may try to use both images, so it sees double versions of objects. Or, it may learn to ignore one eye's input to avoid seeing double. People who are not cross-eyed

Strabismus is when a human's two eyes don't look in the same direction at the same time.

sometimes cross their eyes on purpose for a few moments, just for fun. It is a myth that their eyes will get stuck that way.

Amblyopia, or "lazy eye," is when the brain ignores the information it gets from one eye. One cause of amblyopia is strabismus. Another cause is having good eyesight out of one eye, while the other eye is very farsighted or nearsighted. The brain learns to ignore the eye with poor sight. As the brain ignores one eye's view, objects look flat instead of three-dimensional. This makes it hard to judge distances, which can interfere with playing sports, riding a bike, or driving a car. Lazy eye usually begins in infancy or early childhood. The problem can be improved with help from an eye doctor if caught at an early age.

DOUBLE VISION

Double vision, or **diplopia**, is when people see two copies of objects right next to each other. This can happen for many reasons. If the cornea or the lens gets injured, becomes cloudy, or gets infected with germs, light rays entering the eye are blocked or bent incorrectly. Infection or injury of the optic nerve can cause double vision. Weak or injured eye muscles can also lead to double vision, if both eyes are unable to look in exactly the same direction at the same time. Finally, a brain injury or infection, or diseases such as brain cancer, can hinder the brain's ability to blend the images it receives from each eye into one image.

Famous People with Vision Problems

Andrea Bocelli (born 1958)—With one of the most admired singing voices in the world, as well as skill at playing several musical instruments, Bocelli became blind at age twelve after being hit in the head with a soccer ball.

Ella Fitzgerald (1917–1996)—A world-famous jazz singer, Fitzgerald won numerous awards and praise for her expressive voice and energy. She went blind in her older years because she had **diabetes**, which damages the retinas.

Galileo Galilei (1564–1642)—The famous Italian scientist and philosopher is perhaps best known for his contributions to astronomy, such as improving telescopes, discovering four of Jupiter's moons, and insisting that Earth revolves around the Sun when people believed it was the other way around. In his older years, Galileo gradually became completely blind.

Helen Keller (1880–1968)—Both blind and deaf due to an illness in infancy, Keller became world famous because of her story of learning to communicate. The first deaf and blind person ever to graduate from college, she became a powerful activist for improving how society treats people with disabilities.

Claude Monet (1840–1926)—A renowned painter and founder of the style of French impressionist painting, Monet's eyesight began to worsen in his sixties. He continued to paint, even after he was almost completely blind.

Franklin Delano Roosevelt (1882–1945)—The thirty-second president of the United States, who had very poor vision, was president longer than anyone in history (four terms in a row) because of his success in helping the country recover from World War II.

Marla Runyan (born 1969)—A marathon runner who became the first legally blind athlete ever to participate in the Olympics, Runyan placed eighth in the 1,500-meter race at the Sydney Olympics in 2000. She had won the same distance race a year earlier at the Pan American Games. She was also the fastest American to run the 2002 New York City Marathon.

Harriet Tubman (1820–1913)—A slave during her childhood, Tubman escaped and fled to Canada, only to return to the United States to help hundreds of other slaves escape on the Underground Railroad. Her vision was damaged after she was badly hurt by a slave owner, but she continued to work for the freedom of African Americans.

Marla Runyan (in front) is an accomplished runner despite being legally blind.

Stevie Wonder (born 1950)—This respected singer-songwriter and record producer, who started recording records at age twelve, became blind shortly after his premature birth. His eyes were damaged because he was kept in an incubator with high amounts of oxygen—a once-common cause of blindness that is now preventable.

Double vision may come and go, or it may become permanent. If it starts suddenly, it can be a sign that something serious is wrong with the eyes or the brain. For instance, double vision can be a sign of a stroke—a life-threatening emergency in which a vessel bringing blood to the brain becomes blocked or the vessel breaks and leaks blood before the blood can get to all parts of the brain. Without enough blood, brain cells start to behave abnormally, and they may die. As brain cells die, a person's life is endangered. In this way, double vision can be a life saver—a warning sign to get a doctor's help immediately.

BLINDNESS

Complete blindness means that the eyes process nothing—not even light. Blindness can be the result of a birth defect—meaning that it is already present at birth—because the eyes have not developed properly. Blindness at birth is not very common. Children who are born legally blind often have other conditions, such as hearing problems or difficulty controlling their muscles. Premature babies (born before a full nine months in the mother's womb) who weigh less than 3 pounds are much more likely to become blind than other babies, although newer medical treatments are helping to prevent that.

Blindness can also happen after birth but still at a young age, before a child has learned much about the world through eyesight. If blindness happens later, it can be easier to adjust to life without sight because there are memories of what things used to look like. People can permanently lose their vision later in life because of eye injury, brain injury, or a disease that harms the eyes or the parts of the brain that handle vision. Many blind people are adults who used to have good vision but got an illness that damaged their eyes.

In adults, the disease diabetes is one of the most common causes of blindness. Diabetes is a condition in which the amount of sugar in the bloodstream stays higher than normal for many months or years. Over time, the excess sugar injures blood vessels in the retina, which can cause some blood vessels to shut down and others to leak. This can damage the retina permanently and cause blindness.

Another cause of blindness, especially in aging adults, is when too much fluid collects inside the eyeball and puts extra pressure on the optic nerve, injuring it. That problem is called **glaucoma**. Simple tests at an eye doctor's office can measure eye pressure to see if glaucoma is developing, and medications can lower eye pressure and decrease the likelihood of vision loss. In another disorder, the lenses can become cloudy over time. Then they act like veils that prevent the person from seeing clearly. This condition, called a **cataract**, can be treated with surgery. The old lens is removed, and a plastic one is put in its place.

Cataracts stop a person from seeing clearly. This image shows what a person with cataracts would see while walking down the street.

People who are not completely blind may still be considered legally blind if their vision is bad enough that they cannot move around and perform daily activities easily. They may be able to tell when it is light or dark, and see shapes and movement, but they do not see clear images. In the United States, the definition of legally blind is that the eyes cannot see better than 20/200 no matter what glasses a person wears. That means that if normally sighted people can clearly see an object that is 200 feet (60.1 m) away, the legally blind person needs to be 20 feet (6.1 m) away (or closer) to see the object equally as clearly. The government helps legally blind people by providing special equipment, money, jobs, education, and other services to allow them to enjoy meaningful lives in spite of their poor vision.

3

THE HISTORY OF VISION DISORDERS AND REMEDIES

In ancient times, people thought that the gods were in charge of one's health. If something went wrong, people said prayers and chants to the gods, sometimes with offerings of foods and riches, in the hopes of curing the ailment. Although prayer can be an important part of healing, many scientific discoveries and inventions have led to cures and corrections of health problems, including vision problems.

LENSES LEAD THE WAY

A landmark invention that helps improve eyesight is the lens. A lens is made of clear glass or plastic with a curved surface. A magnifying glass is an example of a lens. Light rays reflected off an object below the magnifying glass are bent outward as they pass through it. The eye sees an enlarged version of the

An early pair of spectacles from the seventeenth century.

object on the other side of the lens. Lenses can do more than magnify. Depending on their thickness and shape, they can correct nearsightedness, farsightedness, and astigmatism, and they can help train eye muscles to work better.

The first use of a glass lens to aid vision seems to have been a reading stone from around 1000 C.E. This object was like half a glass sphere, curved on one side and flat on the other. The flat side was placed on books or maps to magnify the words and pictures. Glass magnifiers just like these are still available today. It was probably the skilled glassworkers of Venice, Italy, who first crafted reading stones. They also made holders for the stones so that they could be held up—the first handheld magnifying glass.

It is not certain who invented eyeglasses, or spectacles, to be worn on the face. There are comments about such objects in writings from the 1200s and 1300s. For instance, an Italian man named di Popozo is said to have written in 1289, "I am so debilitated by age that without the glasses known as spectacles, I would no longer be able to read or write. These have recently been invented for the benefit of poor old people whose sight has become weak." During the 1300s and 1400s, people tried many different ways of keeping glasses on. Finally, today's eyeglass design—resting the nosepiece on the nose with support from earpieces—became the favored design.

For several hundred years, eyeglasses only corrected farsightedness. It was much later, in the 1500s, that lenses were invented to help nearsighted people see distant objects. Another key invention was bifocals, which are very popular today. On these lenses, the bottom portion aids in close-up viewing, and the top portion aids in long-distance viewing. The famous American inventor and statesman Benjamin Franklin invented bifocals because he needed two sets of glasses—one for close up and another for distance—and he got tired of trading back and forth.

The idea of contact lenses, which fit directly on the eyeball, appeared in the mid-1800s. Inventors experimented with

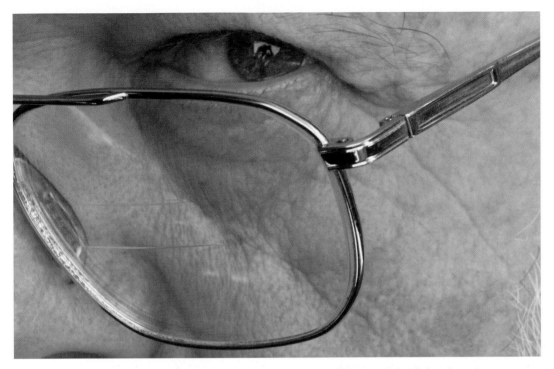

Bifocals combine lenses for people who are both nearsighted and farsighted.

cup-shaped glass lenses for several years. A Swiss doctor, Adolf Eugen Fick, and a German medical student, August Muller, both did studies of patients in the late 1800s to see whether it was possible to wear these lenses without injury. For much of the 1900s, contact lenses were large and not very comfortable. Companies that manufactured contact lenses improved their methods to make the lenses thinner and smaller. Today, many millions of people wear contact lenses. There is even a thin, soft plastic type that can be left on the eyes for many days at a time.

LASIK Surgery

....

About a hundred years ago, doctors started doing surgery on eyes to correct vision problems. Over time, these techniques have improved greatly. Today, thousands of people each year choose to have a simple, painless surgery that changes the shape of the cornea so that it bends light waves a little differently than it used to. That change can correct nearsightedness, farsightedness and astigmatism, and it may make eyeglasses unnecessary. LASIK surgery is done by first numbing the eye with eye drops and then using a laser (a tiny beam of powerful light) to remove a thin layer of the cornea. Once the eye has healed, its shape is improved. Although there can be difficulties in the healing process, most people experience better vision just a day or two after surgery.

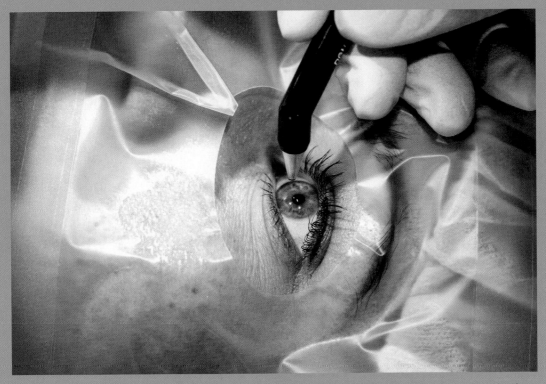

An eye surgeon measures the thickness of a patient's cornea with an ultrasound probe in preparation for LASIK surgery.

EYE SURGERY

A more recent advance in the history of vision correction is eye surgery. Because the eyes are so small compared to many other parts of the body, it takes special equipment and skills for a doctor to perform surgery on the eyes. These methods have been improving for several decades, however, and eye surgeries have become commonplace. Millions of people each year get some sort of surgery to improve their vision or to restore vision that has gotten worse because of disease or injury.

One of the most common eye surgeries is removal of a cataract, or cloudy lens, which causes poor vision or blindness. The lens is carefully removed, and a clear plastic lens is put in its place. After a few days of recovery, people's eyesight is restored. Another common type of eye surgery corrects acuity problems—that is, nearsightedness and farsightedness. The easiest way to do this is to change the shape of the cornea a bit by making it less curved, so that it bends light rays a little differently. For people who are very nearsighted, instead of changing the cornea, a lens can be added to their own eye's lens using surgery. Or, their natural lens can be removed and an artificial lens put in its place.

HELPING THE BLIND

In a world where reading and writing are so important, blindness can be very isolating. Centuries ago, after printing was invented, blind people had to have someone else read to them.

A sheet of paper from a Braille book shows the raised bumps that allow people who are blind to read.

Some of them tried to feel the raised-up ink on pages, but the letters were tiny. A better idea was **Braille**, an alphabet made of raised bumps that a blind person can feel. Braille was invented by Louis Braille, who became blind in an accident at the age of three. In 1829, when Braille was fifteen years old, he created the first Braille system. Each letter was assigned a pattern of raised dots. There were also dot patterns to stand for numbers and punctuation marks. Braille got the idea from a code of punched holes in cards that soldiers on the battlefield used to send messages to one another at night.

Although Braille was a good idea, it was quite a while before books could be easily printed in Braille. A completely different kind of printing press had to be invented. The press pushes raised bumps into paper instead of printing letters in ink. The paper has to be sturdy, and only one side can be used.

Blindness in the Computer Age

The advances of computer technology have not left blind people behind. Many tools have been invented to help blind people enjoy computers even though they cannot see the screen. For instance, computer programs include a voice that reads aloud whatever is on the screen. The programs also turn words that the blind person speaks aloud into written words on the screen. This is one way that a blind person can have online conversations with people.

Another tool for blind people is the Braille printer. It prints out text in Braille, the raised-dot system of language that many blind people learn. Another remarkable invention is a Braille display for the computer. It is a pad that writes out in Braille whatever words are on the computer screen. The pad is like an erasable chalkboard, but instead of using chalk, it "writes" in raised dots that push up into the surface of the pad from below. The pad writes one line at a time, and the blind person can feel the dots to read the text. People who have vision, but very poor close-up focus, can get a large magnifying glass plate that stands in front of their computer screen and enlarges everything. For people who are color blind, a computer program changes green and red colors to patterns that are more noticeable.

Computer companies have created software and hardware for the blind. With the correct tools, the blind can listen to the text on web pages through a special voice interface. A special electronic Braille printer has also been developed.

One of the first books to be printed in Braille was the Bible, which took eight volumes of pages!

Over time, with gradual improvements in printing presses and paper, Braille books became more plentiful. An English version of Braille was developed, and another version called New York Point became popular in the United States. By the late 1800s, Braille was being taught at the St. Louis School for the Blind, and many more books were being printed. There were several versions of Braille at that time, but in 1932, all English-speaking countries agreed to use one system, known as Standard English Braille, Grade 2, which is still used today. Nowadays, millions of pages of materials such as magazines, newspapers, brochures, and books are printed in Braille. Computers do the translating from spoken English, and they are connected to printers that make Braille versions of texts.

Blindness and low vision are different challenges in the twenty-first century than they were long ago. Today, cities are busy, crowded, complex, and sometimes dangerous places that even sighted people can find daunting. On the other hand, there are many computer aids and clever tools to help blind people get around safely and do many things that sighted people do. Special schools and organizations for the blind offer excellent information, training, help with jobs and housing, friendship, and a sense of community. Opportunities for blind and nearly blind people have never been better.

4

DIAGNOSING, TREATING, AND COPING WITH VISION DISORDERS

Many people don't need a test to realize that something is not quite right with their vision. Problems with blurry vision are often first discovered at school, such as when a student has trouble seeing the chalkboard from the back of the room. Many adults discover in middle age (in their forties or fifties) that their close-up vision is getting blurry. Some eye diseases give little warning, however, and only a good eye exam can detect them.

Eye doctors are specialists in checking out how well eyes can see and work together. They also check for health problems related to vision. **Optometrists** and ophthalmologists are eye specialists who can diagnose, or discover, all sorts of vision problems. They also recommend treatments, including glasses, eye exercises, medications, dietary changes, or surgery. Ophthalmologists have medical degrees, just like your family doctor, and some are trained to perform surgery.

VISION TESTING

Vision tests measure what the eyes can and cannot do. The most common type of test is simply reading letters off a chart on the wall at a distance of 20 feet (6.1 m). One eye is covered in order to determine how clearly the other eye sees certain rows of letters. Then the other eye is tested. The chart also has rows of letters that are much smaller than the others, to represent letters even farther away, such as 100 or 200 feet (30 or 60 m). If all rows of letters are easy to read with each eye, then the eyes have perfect acuity, or vision clarity, for distant objects. That is called 20/20 vision, meaning that objects at 20 feet (6.1 m) (and at other distances) look clear.

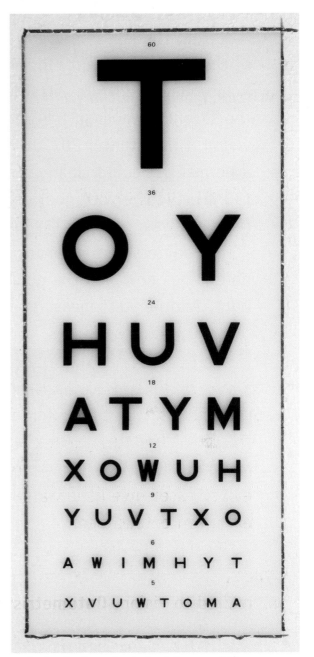

A standard eye test chart is one of the first things optometrists and ophthalmologists use to see if a person has a vision disorder.

Often, though, one eye sees more clearly than the other, or the letters are blurry for both eyes at some of the distances. Acuity may be 20/40, 20/100, 20/200, and so on. The bigger the second number in the fraction, the worse the distance vision. For instance, 20/100 means that to see things that a normal eye could clearly see from a distance of 100 feet (30 m), the eye with poor acuity must be no more than 20 feet (6.1 m) away.

Eye doctors perform many additional tests. One simple test determines how well the pupils change size in bright or dim light. Another test measures how well the eye muscles work to

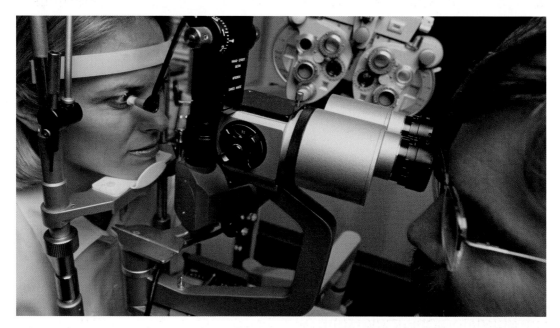

Advanced testing may be necessary after an eye doctor has determined if a person has a vision disorder.

move the eyeballs as they follow, or track, moving objects. Eye doctors also check for how well eyes can see images and movements to the sides while still looking straight ahead. That ability is called peripheral vision, and it keeps us aware of more than just what the eye is looking at straight on. Color vision may be checked, too, using printed cards with colored patterns that are hard to see unless the retina can detect all colors well.

Several tests check eye health. An instrument blows tiny puffs of air at the eyeball's surface to measure how much pressure each eyeball has inside (a test for glaucoma). In addition, the eye doctor carefully looks at the retina and its blood vessels by shining a light through the pupil. Sometimes eye drops are used to relax the iris and expand the pupil so the eye doctor can see the retina more clearly. Infection, damage, or other problems of the retina can be found this way.

If an eye doctor detects acuity or other vision problems, he or she will decide whether corrective lenses can help or whether a patient should try eye exercises or other kinds of training. In the case of an eye disease, medications or surgery may be necessary.

HELP FOR BLURRY VISION

Nearsightedness, farsightedness, and astigmatism are problems of blurry vision. They can often be corrected easily with glasses or contact lenses. Glasses and contact lenses are made specifically for each person to bend light rays just the right amount so that the image on the retina becomes clear. An **optician** is a specialist who provides eyeglasses and contact lenses to customers, according to what the person's eye test reveals.

Contact lenses, which come in hard or soft forms, are worn directly on the cornea. They are held in place by a thin film of moisture from the eye (just as a piece of plastic wrap sticks to a moist surface). Not

A pair of eyeglasses or a set of contact lenses is an easy way to fix blurry vision.

everybody can wear contact lenses—and not everyone wants to. It takes care and time to put them in, to take them out, and to keep them clean. But they are extremely popular, especially for people who play sports or simply prefer the way they look without glasses.

CORRECTING AMBLYOPIA

A thorough eye test can determine whether both eyes are contributing images to the brain. If amblyopia, or lazy eye, is discovered at a young age, it is possible to train the brain to use both eyes instead of ignoring one of them. An eye patch that covers the "good" eye for weeks or months makes the brain pay attention to images coming from the "lazy" eye. Special glasses and eye exercises help, too. These efforts to retrain the brain work best at an early age—before age seven or so—while the brain and eyes are still learning to work together. Later than that, it is much harder to get the brain to "see" the lazy eye.

Wearing an eye patch will help train a lazy eye to work just as hard as the normal eye.

TRAINING TO IMPROVE TRACKING

School eye tests usually measure only acuity, not tracking. Children who are slow learners or cannot read well, or who are restless in school, should have a complete eye test to see whether the two eyes are working in unison. Some children who are thought to be poor students have good acuity but poor tracking. That slows them down when reading, because it is hard for them to follow lines of print. Also, some students who get in trouble for behavior problems, such as not paying attention or being disruptive, actually have tracking problems (or other vision problems that have not yet been discovered). It makes sense that if they cannot read well and start falling

Tips for Taking Care of Your Eyes

....

- Wear protective goggles while doing anything that could get dust, chemicals, or bits of material in your eyes. Examples are science, art, and shop classes at school, and mowing the lawn or woodworking at home.
- Wear protective glasses when playing sports in which your eyes could be injured.
- Protect your eyes from the sun's ultraviolet rays by wearing sunglasses that block UV rays of both types (A and B).
- When performing any task that requires close-up viewing, such as reading or working at the computer, give your eyes a rest every twenty minutes or so by taking five minutes to blink a lot and to gaze out a window or toward something distant in the room.
- When using the computer, make sure no glare from lights appear on the computer screen. Turn your monitor to a new angle if necessary.
- Set the features of your computer screen so that the size of words and the brightness of the background are easy to see but not harsh on the eyes.
- Keep a good light by your desk for reading papers or books while using the computer.
- Get eye checkups regularly.

Wearing protective goggles while working with chemicals is necessary in order to protect your eyes.

behind other students, they become restless. Eye doctors and other eye specialists can provide visual exercises and games that improve tracking. Students who improve their tracking skills often do much better in school.

The old saying that carrots are good for your eyes is true! They contain vitamin A, which is a building block that cells of the retina need.

PROPER NUTRITION

It is common knowledge that carrots are good for your eyes. To be more precise, it is the vitamin A in carrots—and in many other orange and deep green vegetables—that is good for eyesight. Vitamin A is a building block that cells of the retina need. They use the vitamin to make visual pigments that capture light. When light falls on the retina, the visual pigments change somewhat in their form, and this acts as a signal that light has hit the cell. That signal is carried to the brain.

Other vitamins and nutrients are essential for good eye health. A diet that is rich in whole grains and dark-colored vegetables and fruits, and is low in fat, sugars, and processed foods, is an important part of good health. Sugar especially is becoming a health problem, as people become accustomed to wanting sweet snacks and beverages several times a day. High sugar levels in the bloodstream gradually damage the retina and may eventually cause blindness.

Diabetes is a common illness in which sugar levels are high. There are actually two forms of the disease. The first results from the damage of an internal organ called the pancreas. The other form, called Type 2, can develop after years of being overweight. Type 2 diabetes is reaching epidemic proportions in the United States and

A Simple Treatment Prevents Blindness

Blindness can happen for many reasons. In some parts of the world, a common cause of blindness is an eyelid infection called trachoma, which is caused by bacteria. The infection makes the eyelids swell, which pushes the eyelashes inward so they rub against the surface of the eye. Over time, this scratches and scars the eyes, leading to blindness. About 11 million people around the world get this infection each year. Most live in overcrowded villages or towns that have unclean water, poor sanitation, and little or no medical care. Doctors have been traveling to these areas to help. They sometimes use surgery to return the shape of the eyelid to normal, but many patients quickly get reinfected. Now doctors are giving patients antibiotic medication to kill remaining germs after the surgery. That very simple step prevents blindness in some people.

in other countries where many people consume high-sugar, high-calorie foods and beverages with little nutrition.

Type 2 diabetes used to be a disease of adults. But in recent decades, many children have become overweight and are developing this preventable illness. No one knows how diabetes will affect the eyesight of those children, but they may experience severe vision problems or blindness early in life. The good news is that moderate exercise just a few times a week, along with a good diet, can sometimes reverse the progress of type 2 diabetes. Exercise can be something as easy and enjoyable as riding a bike, playing ball, dancing, or even cleaning up around the house or out in the yard.

LIVING WITH BLINDNESS

Imagine living on your own when you cannot see. How do you make meals or do the laundry? What if you want to do your own shopping or get a job? How do you get around in a busy city? Blind people do these things and more. They use tools and inventions, as well as smart tricks and careful planning. Some things are easy to do with practice, such as pouring a beverage or walking around the house. But many things take patience, hard work, and courage.

A simple walking stick can make it possible to be out in the world. The stick is used to tap or glide ahead of the person while walking, to be sure the path is clear, and to find steps or

Guide Dogs

Many people enjoy having a dog for a pet. But for a person who is blind or nearly so, a dog can be a pair of eyes and a smart decision maker. Guide dogs are specially trained to help a person who cannot see well. A guide dog wears a special harness with a handle that the person can hold. Beginning as a puppy, the dog is trained for as many as a thousand hours. Guide dogs do such things as walking at the right speed, staying on sidewalks, stopping before curbs and steps, and waiting for traffic to clear or for walk lights to come on before crossing a street. A guide dog must be very smart and must pay attention to its surroundings in order to keep its human safe. And while many ordinary dogs enjoy greeting other dogs and people they meet while on a walk, a guide dog knows to ignore them until the harness is off and playtime begins. Matching a guide dog and a person is done carefully, to be sure that they like each other and work well together. The dog and human partner train together for a while to get used to each other, and also so the human can learn how to understand the dog's many skills. Not surprisingly, the bond between a guide dog and its human is especially strong. Several thousand people in the United States have guide dogs.

Guide dogs are trained to help people with severe vision problems.

There are many special tools the vision impaired can use. This Braille watch helps the blind to tell time.

walls. Guide dogs, or seeing eye dogs, are another aid to help blind people get around. Having a sighted person for a companion works, too. But some blind people are remarkably independent; they learn to do many things on their own.

A new invention that helps with independence is a tool that uses the GPS system. GPS stands for global positioning system, which is a group of satellites that are orbiting Earth. The satellites can communicate with computers and cell phone-like devices on Earth. While walking outdoors, a blind person with such a device can ask the GPS to explain, in a computer voice, exactly where he or she is standing at any moment. GPS can also help guide the person to a destination. This system replaces something that sighted people take for granted—the simple act of looking around at signs and buildings to see where they are.

Special schools and training help blind people learn skills that give them more freedom, while also keeping them safe. Besides living nearly normal lives, blind people do remarkable things. Some play musical instruments far better than most sighted people. Some hike in the outdoors, even in rugged countryside. Some are medal-winning athletes. Many are artists, using touch and textures to guide their work.

BE GOOD TO YOUR EYES

Vision is unlike any other of the body's senses. It is possible to get along without it, but anyone who has good vision may take it for granted. Many simple habits will protect your eyes for decades, such as eating well and wearing protective glasses when doing things that could harm the eyes. It is important to take these steps while your vision is good. For people who are born with vision problems or develop them later in life, there are many ways that vision can be corrected. Nearly everyone can enjoy the unique enrichment that vision brings.

GLOSSARY

acuity—How well the eyeball can make focused images of objects. Examples of poor acuity are nearsightedness and farsightedness.

amblyopia—A condition, sometimes called "lazy eye," in which the brain ignores the images sent by one eye.

astigmatism—A vision problem in which objects at the edges of view are blurry or misshapen, due to an uneven cornea.

Braille—A code of raised bumps that can be felt with the fingertips. It is used to print books and other materials that blind people can read.

cataract—A cloudiness that has formed inside the eye's natural lens.

ciliary muscles—Tiny muscles in the eyeball that change the shape of the lens so that the eye can see clearly at different distances.

color blindness—A vision problem in which certain shades of colors are seen as gray.

cones—Cells of the retina that respond to light of different colors.

conjunctiva—A clear covering over the white part of the eye.

cornea—The eye's clear covering over the iris and pupil. It protects the eye and aids in acuity.

diabetes—A disease in which sugars are not properly used by the body.

diplopia—Double vision; seeing two images of a single object.

eye socket—The cup-shaped area of the skull that surrounds most of the eyeball.

farsighted—Able to see things clearly in the distance, but not close up.

glaucoma—A disease of the eye in which there is increased pressure within the eyeball, which may damage the retina.

hyperopia—Farsightedness.

iris—The eye's colored ring, made of muscles that change the amount of light that gets through the iris's center (the pupil) and into the eye.

lens—A pea-size, flattened sphere of clear material through which light passes and is focused onto the retina.

myopia—Nearsightedness.

nearsighted—Able to see close-up things clearly, but not things in the distance.

ophthalmologist—A medical doctor who specializes in diagnosing and treating problems related to eye diseases and disorders.

optic nerve—A bundle of nerve cells that connects the back of each eye to the brain and carries information about images that fall on the retina.

optician—A person trained in providing eyeglasses and contact lenses based on a prescription provided by an optometrist or ophthalmologist.

optometrists—A specialist in detecting vision problems and treating them with corrective lenses.

pupil—The opening in the center of the iris that controls how much light passes into the eye.

retina—The back surface of the eyeball's interior, made of light-sensitive cells that convert focused light into nerve impulses.

rods—Cells of the retina that respond to different brightness levels of light.

sclera—The eye's tough protective coating around the iris, also called the white of the eye.

strabismus—An imbalance in the eye muscles, resulting in one eye looking in a different direction than the other.

vitreous humor—The clear jelly that fills the eyeball.

FIND OUT MORE

Books

Cline-Ransome, Lesa. *Helen Keller: The World in Her Heart*. New York: Collins, 2008.

Kirkland, Kyle. *Light and Optics*. New York: Facts on File, 2007.

Websites

American Foundation for the Blind
http://www.afb.org

Centers for Disease Control and Prevention: Vision Impairment
http://www.cdc.gov/ncbddd/dd/ddvi.htm

KidsHealth: Your Eyes
http://kidshealth.org/kid/htbw/eyes.html

INDEX

Page numbers for illustrations are in **boldface.**

acuity, 19, 40, 45–46, 49
aging, 10, 14, 16, 31
astigmatism, 23, 35, 38, 47–48

babies, **24**, 26, 30
bifocals, 36, **37**
birth defects, 29, 30
blindness, 28–31, 33, 40–43, 53, 54–57
blood vessels, 11, 15, 30, 31, 47
blurry vision, 10, 21–24, 44, 46, 47–48
Bocelli, Andrea, 28
Braille, **41**, 41, 42, 43, **56**
brain, 15, 19, 20, 25, 26, 52
    damage to, 10, 27, 30, 31
    training, 24, 48–49

carrots, 52, **52**
cataracts, 31, **32**, 40
color blindness, 16, 42
colors, seeing, 15, 19, 47
computer technology, **42**, 42, 43
cone cells, **14**, 15, 16, 19
conjunctiva, 12, 25
contact lenses, 10, 36–37, 47–48
corneas, 12–13, **13**, 14, **17**, 17, 23, 27
    correcting, 38, 40, 48
crossed eyes (strabismus), **26**, 26–27
crying, 25

diabetes, 28, 31, 53–54
diseases, 10, 16, 21, 27–28, 31, 40, 47,
    53–54
double vision (diplopia), 27, 30

exercises, 49, 52, 54
eyeballs/eyes, **12**, **13**, **18**, **20**, 20–21, **22**
    caring for, 50, **51**, 52–54, 57

movement of, 15, 23–24, 26–27,
    46–47, 49, 52
pressure on, 31, 47
shape of, 10, 23
working of, 11–20, **17**
eye charts, **45**, 45
eye doctors, 44–47, **46**
eyeglasses, **8,** 10, **35**, 36–37, **37**, 47–48,
    48, 49
eyelids, 20, 21, 25, 53
eye patches, 48–49, **49**
eye sockets, 11, 20, 21, 24

farsightedness (hyperopia), 21–23, **22**, 27
    correcting, 35, 36, 38, 40, 42, 47–48
Fick, Adolf Eugen, 37
Fitzgerald, Ella, 28
Franklin, Benjamin, 36

Galilei, Galileo, 28
glaucoma, 31, 47
global positioning systems (GPS), 56–57
goggles, 50, **51**
guide dogs, 55, **55**

heredity, 10, 16

injuries, 27, 30, 31, 40
irises, 11–12, **12**, **13**, 13, 47

Keller, Helen, 28

LASIK surgery, 38, **39**
lazy eyes (amblyopia), 27, 48–49
lenses (corrective). *See* contact lenses;
    eyeglasses; magnifying glasses
lenses (part of eye), **13**, **17**, 27, 31, 40
    working of, 13–14, 17–18, 19, 21, 23
light/light rays, 12, 14, 15, **17**, 52
    bending, 17–18, 21, 23, 27, 34, 40,
    48
magnifying glasses, 34–35, 36, 42

Monet, Claude, 28
Muller, August, 37
muscles, 11, **20**, 20, 24, 26, 35, 46–47
ciliary, 13–14, 19
nearsightedness (myopia), 21–23, **22**, 27
    correcting, 35, 36, 38, 40, 47–48
nutrition, 10, 52–54

optic nerves, **13**, **14**, 15, **20**, 20, 27, 31

peripheral vision, 47
pupils, 11–12, **12**, **13**, 13, 15, **17**, 17,
    46, 47

retinas, **13**, **14**, 14–15, 31, 47, 53
    working of, 17, **17**, 19, 21–23, **22**, 48, 52
rod cells, **14**, 14–15
Roosevelt, Franklin Delano, 29
Runyan, Maria, **29**, 29

sclera, 11, **12**, 12, **13**
spectacles. *See* eyeglasses
strokes, 30
sugar, 31, 53, 54
surgery, 38–39, 40

tear glands, 25
testing vision, **16**, **45**, 45–47, **46**, 48, 49
three-dimensional vision, 19–20
trachoma, 53
tracking, 23–24, 26, 49, 52
Tubman, Harriet, 29

Vitamin A, 52

Wonder, Stevie, 29

ABOUT THE AUTHOR

Lorrie Klosterman is a biologist who writes and teaches college courses about health, the human body, and nature. Other books she has written for Benchmark Books include the Health Alert titles *Leukemia*, *Meningitis*, and *Rabies*.